Descriptosaurus Punctuation in Action Year 3: Ruby Red

You've heard of Little Red Riding Hood – now meet her cousin, Ruby Red, who makes the same journey through the forest to visit her granny. However, Ruby Red's story takes a strange turn when she also meets a wolf in the forest. In grave danger, lost in the dark forest and sick from eating poisonous berries, Ruby learns the importance of listening to her parents, keeping her promises and not judging everyone by the actions of one member of a group.

Join Ruby on her journey as she writes the story of her meeting with the wolf and as she learns with the assistance of the wolf and Punctua, the Fairy Godmother of Writing, to punctuate properly and become a bestselling author.

Descriptosaurus Punctuation in Action Year 3: Ruby Red is part of a short series of age-specific, beautifully illustrated stories that can be read for pleasure and/or used as a contextualised resource, containing a step-by-step guide to teaching punctuation. The characters from each story are used to demonstrate a range of punctuation rules in a fun and engaging way appropriate to the book's age group. Areas covered include:

★ formulating punctuation rules.
★ the use of misconceptions to highlight common errors.
★ teaching tips to provide a punctuation model.

The book explores the impact of punctuation on reading, understanding, meaning and effect, and can be used as a basis for pupils' own punctuation or included in their "Writer's Toolkit." These new *Descriptosaurus* stories are an indispensable teaching aid for making punctuation fun for all primary teachers and literacy coordinators.

Alison Wilcox is the author of the *Descriptosaurus* series and has worked as a primary school teacher for many years. Whilst teaching, she developed *Descriptosaurus* to scaffold and improve children's creative writing, with dramatic results, and she made the decision to give up full-time teaching to work on the *Descriptosaurus* series. To keep up to date with current practices in schools, Alison undertakes brief teaching assignments, works with schools to develop new resources and conducts workshops for schools and teaching alliances.

Descriptosaurus Punctuation in Action Year 3

Ruby Red

Alison Wilcox

Routledge
Taylor & Francis Group
LONDON AND NEW YORK

First published 2022
by Routledge
2 Park Square, Milton Park, Abingdon, Oxon OX14 4RN

and by Routledge
605 Third Avenue, New York, NY 10158

Routledge is an imprint of the Taylor & Francis Group, an informa business

British Library Cataloguing-in-Publication Data
A catalogue record for this book is available from the British Library

Library of Congress Cataloging-in-Publication Data
Names: Wilcox, Alison, author.
Title: Descriptosaurus punctuation in action year 3: Ruby Red/Alison Wilcox.
Description: Abingdon, Oxon; New York: Routledge, 2021. |
Identifiers: LCCN 2021008198 | ISBN 9781032040868 (hardback) |
ISBN 9781032040875 (paperback) | ISBN 9781003190479 (ebook)
Subjects: LCSH: English language–Punctuation–Study and teaching (Elementary). |
Conduct of life–Juvenile literature.
Classification: LCC PE1450 .W46 2021 | DDC 428.2/3–dc23
LC record available at https://lccn.loc.gov/2021008198

ISBN: 978-1-032-04086-8 (hbk)
ISBN: 978-1-032-04087-5 (pbk)
ISBN: 978-1-003-19047-9 (ebk)

DOI: 10.4324/9781003190479

Typeset in MyridPro
by Deanta Global Publishing Services, Chennai, India

Contents

Dedication and acknowledgement

I would like to dedicate this book to all those wonderful teachers I have met and worked with who, despite any curriculum or assessment limitations, remain committed to finding creative ways of teaching.

Thanks as always to my family for all their support and encouragement, and for being patient and understanding when I 'disappear into my fictional worlds.' A special thanks to my daughter, Kitty, for reading, reviewing and proofreading *Ruby Red*, and to my mother, Ann, who laughed in all the right places.

Thanks to Adam Bushnell. When you share a real joy of teaching and learning and get a fizz in the stomach when you see pupils getting excited about writing, you know you've chosen the right person with whom to collaborate.

Over 12 years ago, Bruce Roberts of Routledge took a chance on me as an author and *Descriptosaurus* as a concept. I am still indebted to him for his belief, encouragement and wise guidance.

Thanks to Molly Selby of Routledge for keeping us on track. Your support and efficiency are invaluable to completing the projects.

Huge thanks to the amazing and talented illustrators Nigel Clifton and Dani Pasteau for their contribution to this book.

Introduction

Research has demonstrated the negative impact SPAG (spelling, punctuation and grammar) has had on creativity. It has also revealed that the knowledge and application required in the context of the test have not resulted in a marked improvement in the quality of pupils' written texts as it is decontextualised and places emphasis primarily on identification and labelling. It does not, therefore, equip young writers to apply their knowledge of punctuation in their own writing, or, more specifically, assist them in developing a system for editing their own texts. In response, the new Ofsted Framework has focused on being able to demonstrate pupil progress in the writing process, which includes pupils being able to revise and edit their own written work.

Resources are, therefore, required to demonstrate models and support pupils with understanding the editing process, as well as developing their knowledge of writing conventions. In addition to providing models in the context of a short story, there is a need for young writers to be able to investigate, discuss and explore texts to assess the impact of punctuation on the reading and understanding of a text.

Whilst most punctuation resources provide models, it is a useful exercise for pupils to be presented with incorrect punctuation so that they can begin to understand the importance of communicating a clear meaning and can use that knowledge and understanding when editing their own texts. Each of the punctuation sections in these short stories will examine rules, misconceptions and common errors as well as providing punctuation models.

The *Descriptosaurus: Punctuation in Action* series are companion books to *Descriptosaurus Story Writing: Language in Action*, which was designed to combine the need to develop descriptive vocabulary for a wide range of settings and characters with models of story and sentence structure, and grammar, as well as exercises to scaffold pupils as they innovate and invent their own models. There are four stories in the series: *The Ninjabread Girl*, *Captain Moody and His Pirate Crew*, *Ruby Red* and *Jack and the Crystal Fang*. Each story has been written in a different style and with the curriculum needs of each year group in mind. The individual stories can be used, innovated and deconstructed according to the level, experience and knowledge of each age group, class or individual.

The story of *Ruby Red* can be used for "reading for pleasure," but also contains a section on punctuation. The aim is to demonstrate punctuation in the context of a story and with characters that will have become familiar from reading the story. The characters are used to demonstrate a range of punctuation rules appropriate to the targeted age group:

1. formulating punctuation rules
2. using misconceptions to highlight common errors
3. using teaching tips to provide a punctuation model

They can be used as a basis for pupils' own punctuation posters and cards, or copied to include in their 'Writer's Toolkit.'

RUBY RED

Part A: The story of Ruby Red

You've heard of Little Red Riding Hood – now meet her cousin, Ruby Red, who makes the same journey through the forest to visit her granny. However, Ruby Red's story takes a strange turn when she also meets a wolf in the forest. In grave danger (lost in the dark forest and sick from eating poisonous berries) Ruby learns the importance of listening to her parents, keeping her promises and not judging everyone by the actions of one member of a group.

Part B: Learning punctuation with the characters

Join Ruby on her journey as she writes the story of her meeting with the wolf, and how she learns, with the assistance of the wolf and Punctua (the Fairy Godmother of Writing), to punctuate properly and become a bestselling author.

Part A
The story of Ruby Red

1

Ruby Red

DOI: 10.4324/9781003190479-1

My name is Ruby Red, and I live in '*once upon a time*' in a village on the edge of a forest. You've probably heard of my cousin, Little Red Riding Hood. She was the one who got into a bit of bother with a wolf.

Like Little Red Riding Hood, or RRH for short, I also wear red, but then so do my father, mother, brother, uncle and aunt. Granny got a huge discount on a large roll of red cloth and has been making us all revolting red clothes for the past year. I really *hate* red! I look like a rotten radish.

Anyway, back to my story.

Like RRH, I also go to visit Granny and walk through the forest to take her a scrumptious picnic basket of homemade goodies. And like RRH, I once met a wolf. Luckily, it didn't eat me all up.

But I must tell you, my story ended very, very differently from my cousin's.

2

The forest

DOI: 10.4324/9781003190479-2

The day it happened was sunny and the forest was covered in beautiful bright sunlight. It had been raining for days, so I was glad to get out of the house. Mother had given me the usual warnings, "Don't talk to strangers. Go straight to Granny's and don't wander off the path. Watch out for any wolves." I intended to keep my promise, but as often happens, I soon forgot.

I set off following the narrow, twisting path through the forest. I took deep breaths of the wonderful, fragrant scents of summer drifting through the air. Above me, in the treetops, the birds were singing. Everywhere I looked there was a rainbow of bright colours. Petals like pink confetti were scattered over the ground. Enormous groups of red, purple and white blossoms hung from the branches. Vivid, lime green vines wound around the huge tree trunks.

I hadn't walked far when I spotted a clearing full of dazzling purple and white flowers like a carpet of glittering jewels. Granny loves flowers, so I decided to pick her a bunch. Somewhere in the back of my mind, I seemed to remember my mother telling me not to pick wildflowers, but these flowers didn't look very wild. So, I set off through the forest towards the clearing.

As I walked through the forest, I could hear the leaves rustling all around me. I stopped for a moment and sat on a log to watch the birds. I listened to the cheerful chattering of the magpies and saw them busily fluttering from tree to tree to hide their stolen treasure.

I hadn't intended to stay long, but I was fascinated by the squirrels. Up and down, up and down they scampered and then sat on a branch to nibble at the nuts clutched between their tiny fingers.

I don't know how long I had been sat on the log, but my tummy started to rumble. I must have missed my lunch! I was tempted to have a nibble of the loaf of bread in my picnic basket, but Mum would be really furious if she found out.

"Time to get moving," I thought. I set off back to the path, but out of the corner of my eye, I spotted clusters of bright berries hanging from the bushes. I could hear my mother's warning, "Do not eat anything in the forest because it might be poisonous and make you very sick." But I was really hungry, and the berries looked scrumptious. "I'll try one. One can't make me sick," I thought. So, off I went.

I picked the biggest, plumpest, brightest berry you have ever seen and popped it into my mouth. Immediately, a yummy, sweet syrup exploded in my mouth and trickled down my fingers and chin. They were the sweetest, juiciest berries I had ever tasted, so I picked another and another until they had all gone. My fingers and face were stained with sticky red juice. "Oh, no! Mum will definitely know I've been eating berries now," I yelped. Quickly, I licked my sticky fingers and tried to scrub the juice off my face. My mum could get very, very cross. I should know. I've been in trouble often enough.

3

The berries

DOI: 10.4324/9781003190479-3

I had been so busy following the berry bushes, I hadn't noticed that I had walked deeper and deeper into the forest. Above my head, the trees were knotted together in a dark arch. Misty light shone through gaps in the trees and it made them look like ghostly statues. I was sure I had seen shadowy figures dancing wildly on the path in front of me.

I looked around nervously and tried to find something familiar to guide me back to the path. It was a total nightmare! I got terribly lost because I wandered around and around in circles. I ended up in a part of the forest I had never seen before. I was scratched and bruised. I couldn't see the tangled roots twisting and wriggling across the ground, and they kept tripping me up.

This part of the forest was deathly quiet, so every sound made me jump out of my skin. My heart was leaping like a salmon in my chest. I started to walk faster and faster, but I soon had to slow down because sharp thorns kept leaping out of the tangle of trees and bushes and grabbing at my coat and skirt.

I was sure I was being followed and kept looking over my shoulder. Suddenly, I heard the snap of a twig and froze. My eyes darted left and right as I tried to catch sight of any movement, but I couldn't see a thing. By now, not only was my heart thudding but there was also sweat streaming down my back. My hands were sweaty, and I kept having to rub them dry on my skirt.

My tummy had been making some very strange noises for a while and all of a sudden, a terrible pain tore through my stomach. I yelled in agony, bent over and clutched my stomach. Wave after wave of agony rose through my body and I felt really sick. I tried to keep on walking, but it was no good. Finally, I gave up and slumped onto my knees. I wrapped my arms tightly around my middle and groaned and groaned and groaned.

Soon, the pain was unbearable and when I tried to stand up my head began to swim. I shouted, "Help me, somebody! Is there anybody there? Help!" I waited and waited, and screamed and screamed until my throat was sore, but no one came.

Suddenly, I started to heave and retch. And then, bright red berry juice erupted in a frothy fountain from my mouth. Sweat poured down my forehead into my eyes, but I didn't have time to wipe it away. A wave of horrific pain like a clenched fist punched me in the stomach. When I retched, another stream of berry juice exploded from my mouth. I was sweating and shivering at the same time. My head was on fire.

Whenever I tried to stand up, my knees gave way and I ended up in a heap on the floor. I had to keep my eyes shut because every time I opened them the world spun madly round and round. Finally, the streams of berry juice vomit stopped, and I lay down and curled into a ball.

4

The wolf

DOI: 10.4324/9781003190479-4

I drifted in and out of sleep. I had a strange feeling that something or someone kept trying to wake me up. I thought I'd felt a warm breath on my cheek, but I couldn't open my eyes to look. Then, I felt something wiry tickle my face. Next, a nibble on my arm. Finally, I was jolted fully awake by a wet nuzzling on my fingers. I forced one eye open and glanced to the right. Standing over me was a wolf.

"Dragon's dung! I really should have listened to my mother," I moaned. By now, I was resigned to my fate. I had no energy to run. I closed my eyes again and rolled over.

"Yes, dear girl. You should have listened to your mother. Never eat anything from the forest," a deep voice boomed.

"Oh, help! Now I'm dreaming a wolf is talking to me," I wailed and pressed my hands over my ears.

"Ouch!" I yelped. The wolf had nipped my hand.

"Come on. Get up. If you lie there much longer you will die from the poison and the cold."

Slowly, I raised myself up onto my elbows. The wolf was sitting beside me and instead of snarling fangs, I was looking into a pair of gentle amber eyes.

"Little girl, I am not going to eat you. Not all wolves try to eat little girls you know. I came because I knew you were in trouble."

"I don't understand," I said, puzzled. "A wolf ate my Granny and tried to eat my cousin."

"That would be my uncle. He was the wicked wolf of the family. He was the one who went around blowing down little pigs' houses, eating grannies and dressing up in their clothes. Because of him, wolves have an awfully bad name. We're not safe anywhere now."

"But isn't he dead?" I asked.

"Thankfully, yes! A terrible end really. First, he was boiled in a pot by the pigs and left with terrible burns all over his body. And that's why he stole your granny's clothes – to hide the scars. Finally, he lost his head to a woodcutter. And that was the end of him."

"I'll tell everyone you saved my life and then we'll be friends," I said excitedly.

"They'll never believe you. If you tell them you met me, we will be driven out of the forest again. They'll never understand that wolves only attack humans if we are threatened. We have never *ever* eaten humans. We're partial to a chicken, the odd rabbit and a fish, but human flesh is tough and chewy like leather, so I've heard." I was sure I heard the wolf chuckle.

"They will listen to me, I promise," I begged.

"No! Swear to me that you will never tell anyone of our meeting," he growled.

"I promise," I said, but I did have my fingers crossed behind my back. That's why I can share this story with you.

Suddenly, I saw the wolf's nose twitch and his ears flick forward. He sniffed the air and his body tensed.

"It's time to get you back to your parents, Ruby. They are looking for you. I can hear them shouting your name."

I hadn't heard anything, but I know wolves can hear things miles away.

The wolf crouched down. I clambered up onto his warm, grey back and held on tightly to his fur. He rose under me and shot off through the trees, threading his way between the tree trunks and leaping over fallen logs. Soon, we were back at the path and I could now hear my father's voice calling my name.

The wolf crouched down again and lowered me to the ground. "This is where I leave you. Remember your promise, Ruby. Never tell anyone that we met." He turned and raced back towards the trees.

He had just disappeared into the shadows when I saw my mother and father racing towards me. There was a lot of crying and hugging and my father carried me home. Later, there was a lot of scolding, a few punishments and some really disgusting medicine like bitter, black liquorice syrup.

In the past, I may not have kept my promises, but I now try very hard not to break a promise. I will never again eat anything from the forest unless it is given to me by a grown-up. I often wonder if the wolf would have become my friend if I'd kept my promise and not told anyone that I had met him in the forest. Every time I walk through the forest, I look for the wolf. Sometimes, I think I catch a brief glimpse of him, but since that day we have never met again.

Part B

Learning punctuation with the characters

5

Meet the characters

Section 1: Ruby Red

Section 2: The Wolf (Lord of Lupus Forest)

Section 3: Punctua (the Fairy Godmother of Writing)

DOI: 10.4324/9781003190479-5

SECTION 1: RUBY RED

Hi, I'm Ruby, the author of this story. I am delighted with the published story, and hope you enjoyed reading it as much as I enjoyed writing it.

I want to say a huge thank you to Punctua, my fairy godmother. Without her assistance, I wouldn't have been able to turn my exciting ideas into a fabulous story that I hope you found easy to read, understand and enjoy.

Whilst the wolf was irritating, as he picked up all my mistakes, his comments were actually very useful to show me that it is important to punctuate my writing correctly so that my readers can enjoy the story.

SECTION 2: THE WOLF (LORD OF LUPUS FOREST)

Mr Wolf refused to give an interview, but issued the following statement:

Ruby left the first draft of her story in the hollow of the old oak tree. I only managed the first page, and that took me ages to read. My first thought was, "This girl should spend less time visiting her granny and more time in the classroom." However, I admit that now she has learned how to edit it correctly, it is a good, well-written story.

I would add that she did exaggerate how sick she was after eating the berries, and I'm still furious that she didn't keep her promise and told everyone about our meeting. I have been plagued by reporters ever since.

Mr Wolf (Lord of Lupus Forest)

SECTION 3: PUNCTUA (THE FAIRY GODMOTHER OF WRITING)

Greetings, readers. I'm Punctua, the Fairy Godmother of Writing. I have worked with all the famous authors over many centuries.

Ruby was a delight to work with. Her ideas were brilliant, and she was keen to learn how to make them clear, exciting, and easy to read and understand.

She worked hard every day learning about punctuation until her story was edited correctly and ready for publication and performance. She thoroughly deserves all her success. Well done, Ruby, on becoming an international bestselling author.

Punctua

6

Editing a story

Section 1: Writing and editing tips

Section 2: Sentences

Section 3: Comma splicing

DOI: 10.4324/9781003190479-6

SECTION 1: WRITING AND EDITING TIPS

Editing a story

The process:

★ Write a first draft.

★ Edit: check grammar, spelling and punctuation.

RUBY'S WRITING TIPS:

When I have a really good story to tell, the words in my head want to spill onto the page. If I stop to think about spelling and punctuation, I forget what I wanted to write. It's more like the words trickle out of my head like a leaky tap.

The best way for me is to "spill" my story onto the page and when I have finished it, read it aloud, either to myself or to Punctua. This makes it easier to spot when it doesn't make sense and I need to insert punctuation marks.

Sometimes, Lord Lupus reads my writing aloud to me, cocks his eyebrow when it clearly doesn't make sense (which I find a bit off-putting, to be honest), but it does help me to hear where my writing isn't clear and needs some punctuation.

To help me with my editing, I make little punctuation rule cards and include a number of examples.

Ruby xx

PUNCTUA'S POINTS:

When you are editing your writing, **read it aloud** and:

★ note when you **pause.**

★ put a pencil mark at that point on your text.

Ask:

★ Why did I **pause**?

★ Was it because:

   a. the thought, statement, idea or description was **complete**?

   b. you had to re-read what was written because it **didn't make any sense**?

RUBY'S FIRST DRAFT:

my name is ruby red and
I live in marston it is a little
village on the edge of
the forest

Editing a story

The first draft:

Read it aloud.

Does it make sense?

Check full stops and capital letters.

WOLF'S WHINES:

What does this mean? It doesn't make any sense. They are *not* sentences.

I'm finding it too hard to read and understand.

PUNCTUA'S POINTS:

Punctuation is a series of traffic signals. Without it, words bang together, and your writing won't make any sense. It will take your reader a long time to get to the end and they could get terribly lost.

A **full stop** is the most important **punctuation mark**. It helps you to **signal to your reader** that the **sentence has ended**, and the statement (thought, description, idea) is **complete**.

When reading your first draft, ask yourself these questions:

1. Is this a sentence?
2. Does it make **sense**?
3. Is it **complete** or do extra words need to be added?
4. Does it start with a **capital letter** and end with a **full stop**?

In Ruby's first draft, there were no full stops or capital letters, and no complete sentences.

my name is Ruby Red and I live in marston it is a little village on the edge of the forest

1. We need a **capital letter** at the start – **My** – and a **full stop** at the end.
2. Where is the first complete statement? My name is Ruby Red.
3. Where is the second complete statement? I live in Marston.
4. Where is the third complete statement? It is a little village on the edge of the forest.

Note: Ruby has joined the first two statements with **and** to **combine them into one sentence**.

So, the first complete sentence should have been:

My name is Ruby Red, and I live in Marston.

SECTION 2: SENTENCES

Sentences

There are four types of sentences:

- ★ Statement (.)
- ★ Question (?)
- ★ Command/instruction (.)
- ★ Exclamation (!)

RUBY'S RULES:

A frothy fountain of bright red berry juice erupted from my mouth. **(statement)**

I really hate red! **(exclamation)**

Is a wolf really talking to me? **(question)**

Get up before you die from the cold. **(command)**

WOLF'S WHINES:

But in Ruby' first draft she thought a sentence ended in a full stop, regardless of whether it was a statement, question or exclamation.

PUNCTUA'S POINTS:

Remember: punctuation marks are a series of traffic signals.

Punctuation marks make it **easier to read** and **understand what has been written** and **how** it is meant to be **read** or **spoken**.

(There are more tips about question marks and exclamation marks later.)

It is true to say that **every sentence ends with a full stop**.

Look closely at the **bottom** of a **question mark** and an **exclamation mark**. What do you notice?

Both have a full stop at the bottom!

Recap:

A **sentence** is a **unit of words** that is **complete** and **makes sense**.

It can be a **statement**, **question**, **exclamation** or **instruction**.

A **sentence** always **starts** with a **capital letter** and **ends** with a **full stop**.

SECTION 3: COMMA SPLICING

Comma splicing

- ★ Commas cannot be used to join two complete sentences.
- ★ Use a conjunction to join two sentences instead.

RUBY'S RULES:

Sometimes two **sentences** link ideas, thoughts or descriptions and you want to join the sentences together.

A comma *cannot* be used to join two sentences. This is called **comma splicing**.

You need to use a **conjunction** to link the two sentences.

My knees gave way**, and**
I ended up in a heap on the floor.

WOLF'S WHINES:

I *really* hate comma splicing. It is painful to read.

Ruby spliced so many sentences in her first draft, it was carnage. She wrote:

> My knees gave way, I ended up in a heap on the floor, I couldn't move.
>
> My uncle had terrible burns, he stole your granny's clothes.

36 *Editing a story*

PUNCTUA'S POINTS:

For your writing to flow and not sound jerky, it is important to **vary the length of your sentences**.

But **two complete sentences cannot be joined by a comma**.

You need to use a **conjunction**, for example: **and**, **but**, **so**, **or**.

When editing your writing, *check*:

★ how many complete statements are included in one sentence?
★ have you joined them using a comma or a conjunction?

Examples:

We can link two sentences to:

1. **add another statement** using **and**.
   My knees gave way, **and** I ended up in a heap on the floor.
2. **add a different option** using **but**.
   I took deep breaths, **but** I couldn't stop the frothy fountain of pink berry juice exploding out of my mouth.
3. **explain the first statement** using **so**.
   My uncle had terrible burns, **so** he stole your granny's clothes to cover them up.

7

Capital letters

Section 1: Beginning of a sentence and names of people

Section 2: Names of places

Section 3: Days of the week and months of the year

Section 4: Editing checklist

DOI: 10.4324/9781003190479-7

SECTION 1: BEGINNING OF A SENTENCE AND NAMES OF PEOPLE

Capital letters

- ★ start every sentence.
- ★ are used for names of people.

RUBY'S RULES:

Capital letters are used:

- ★ to start a sentence.
- ★ for the names of people.
- ★ for 'I.'

Examples:

My name is **R**uby **R**ed. **I** met the wolf on the way to visit **G**ranny.

WOLF'S WHINES:

In the first draft, there were no capital letters for the names of people. Ruby wrote **ruby red** and **little red riding hood**. If I hadn't known better, I would have assumed it was a colour, not a person, and a small hood that you attached to a coat when you rode a horse.

By the way, my name is Lord Lupus.

PUNCTUA'S POINTS:

Capital letters are **signposts** that help us to understand a text, spot the **characters** and **places** easily.

Ruby remembered to **start her sentences** with a capital letter, and she remembered a capital letter for '**I**.'

However, she forgot about the **names of people**.

Ruby Red and **Little Red Riding Hood** both start with a capital letter, as do **Punctua**, **Lord Lupus** and **Granny**.

SECTION 2: NAMES OF PLACES

Capital letters

- ★ start every sentence.
- ★ are used for names of people and 'I.'
- ★ are used for names of places.

RUBY'S RULES:

Capital letters are used for:

★ names of **places**.

Examples:

I live in a village called **M**arston on the edge of the **L**upus **F**orest.

WOLF'S WHINES:

Ruby's first draft had no capital letters for places. She wrote:

I live in a village called Marston on the edge of the lupus forest. To get to Granny's house, I cross over the river wharfe to rathbottom, then turn right to wigglesworthy.

I wouldn't be able to find her Granny's house from those directions.

PUNCTUA'S POINTS:

Capital letters are **signposts** that help us to spot the **names of places** easily.

Ruby remembered that her village, **Marston**, started with a capital letter because she sees it every day when she leaves the village.

However, she forgot that the **forest** has a name, as does the **river**, and **rathbottom** and **wigglesworthy** are the names of other **villages**.

She should have written:

I live in a village called **M**arston on the edge of the **L**upus **F**orest. To get to **G**ranny's house, I cross over the **R**iver **W**harfe to **R**athbottom, then turn right to **W**igglesworthy.

SECTION 3: DAYS OF THE WEEK AND MONTHS OF THE YEAR

Capital letters

1. start every sentence.
2. are used for:
   - ★ names of people and 'I.'
   - ★ names of places.
   - ★ days of the week.
   - ★ months of the year.

RUBY'S RULES:

Capital letters are important. They **start a sentence** and should be used for:

a. names of **people**, as well as '**I**.'
b. names of **places**.
c. **days** of the week.
d. **months** of the year.

WOLF'S WHINES:

Yes, capitals are important, dear girl! So, don't keep forgetting:

★ days of the week.
★ months of the year.

It's Friday, not friday; June, not june. I thought you were talking about a day when you fried your food. Next, we'll have a boilday!

PUNCTUA'S POINTS:

I gave this model for Ruby to keep in her **Writer's Toolkit**. Whenever she can't remember when to use capital letters, she can use this **model** to help her. It's always useful to have a model to look at when you are editing.

My name is **Ruby Red**. **I** live in a village called **Marston** on the edge of the **Lupus Forest**. **One Friday** in **June**, I persuaded my mother, **Mrs Red**, to let me go to **Granny's** house.

To get to the path that leads to **Granny's** house, I turn left at **Gigglesmouth Station**, then, past my favourite café, **Sugar and Spice**, cross the **River Wharfe** to **Wigglesworthy**. **The** entrance is opposite the **Black Sheep Farm**.

SECTION 4: EDITING CHECKLIST

Capital letters

1. start every sentence.
2. are used for:
   - ★ names of people, including 'I.'
   - ★ names of places.
   - ★ days of the week.
   - ★ months of the year.

EDITING CHECKLIST:

I found it hard to remember where to put capital letters, so Punctua and I came up with this checklist to use when I am editing.

I take each item one at a time:

1. beginning of every sentence ☐
2. names of people ☐
3. 'I.' ☐
4. names of places ☐
5. days of the week ☐
6. months of the year ☐

8

Question marks

DOI: 10.4324/9781003190479-8

Question marks

★ go at the end of direct questions.

RUBY'S RULES:

Question marks go **at the end** of **direct questions**, which usually begin with words like:

Who? What? When?

Why? Where? How?

Is? Are? Can? Will?

WOLF'S WHINES:

What do you call someone who doesn't keep a promise?

Who promised never to tell anyone about our meeting?

Can you ever trust someone who doesn't keep their promises?

Why is the forest surrounded by reporters?

Will Ruby ever learn to listen to her mother?

Who asks lots of questions, but forgets to put a question mark at the end of the question?

PUNCTUA'S POINTS:

Young writers:

- ★ get **direct** and **indirect questions** confused.
- ★ forget the **question mark** at the **end of the sentence**.

Direct question:

- ★ where the speaker's **exact words are repeated**

For example:

What have you eaten**? Who** did you meet**? When** did you get home**?**

Indirect question:

- ★ where the exact words are **not repeated**

For example:

The wolf **asked me** what I had eaten. Mum **asked me** who I had met.

9

Exclamation marks

DOI: 10.4324/9781003190479-9

48 *Exclamation marks*

Exclamation marks

Exclamation marks are used to show:

- ★ surprise.
- ★ an outburst.
- ★ humour.

RUBY'S RULES:

Exclamation marks signal:

- ★ **surprise**: Dragon's Dung, a wolf is talking to me!
- ★ **an outburst**: Ouch! Get off me!
- ★ **humour**: What do you call a talking wolf? Chatty!

WOLF'S WHINES:

Ruby is a very excitable, dramatic young girl. She emphasises *everything*. She shouts and shrieks a lot!

In her first draft, she either forgot to signal a surprise or an outburst by using an exclamation mark, or she put exclamation marks at the end of every sentence, which was really *irritating*!

Did you know exclamation marks were once called *shrieks* – a great name for the noises Ruby makes when she is surprised or scared?

PUNCTUA'S POINTS:

Exclamation marks are a **signal** to the reader that the **character** has a **strong emotional reaction** to something.

It could be:

- ★ a **surprise**.
- ★ an **outburst**.
- ★ a **joke**.

Example:

Dragon's dung**!** A wolf is talking to me**!**

They are extremely useful for **emphasis** but should **not** be used **too often**.

10

Inverted commas (speech marks)

Section 1: When and how to use inverted commas

Section 2: How to punctuate inside the inverted commas

DOI: 10.4324/9781003190479-10

SECTION 1: WHEN AND HOW TO USE INVERTED COMMAS

Inverted commas (speech marks)

Inverted commas (speech marks) are used to:

- ★ identify dialogue (direct speech).
- ★ enclose the exact words spoken.

Use commas to separate speech from the rest of the sentence.

RUBY'S RULES:

- ★ Use **speech marks** to **quote the exact words** someone has **said**.
- ★ Usually use **"double quotation marks"** (*66* and *99*).
- ★ Speech marks are also called **inverted commas**.

Example:
"I can hear your parents shouting your name," said the wolf.

- ★ **the exact words spoken by the wolf**
- ★ enclosed within **speech marks** at the **beginning** and the **end**
- ★ a **comma** separates the words spoken from the rest of the sentence

WOLF'S WHINES:

In the first draft Ruby wrote:

Mother shouted from the door don't talk to strangers.

I had difficulty working out what exactly Ruby's mother had said.

At first, I thought she meant don't talk to strangers from the door.

PUNCTUA'S POINTS:

1. Mother shouted from the door don't talk to strangers.

To ensure that the reader doesn't get confused about **who is talking** and **what they say**, we need to use **speech marks** to **separate the speaker** and **their words**.

"Don't talk to strangers." (This is what Mother said.)

To **separate the speech from the rest of the sentence** and make it clear **what is being said by whom** we **need** a **comma**.

Mother shouted from the door, "Don't talk to strangers."

We could have put the **speech first**, but we still need a **comma** to **separate the speech** and the **speaker**.

"Don't talk to strangers," Mother shouted from the door.

(Note: the comma comes inside the speech marks.)

SECTION 2: HOW TO PUNCTUATE INSIDE THE INVERTED COMMAS

Inverted commas (speech marks)

- ★ The words a person says always begin with a capital letter.
- ★ Question marks and exclamation marks go inside the speech marks.
- ★ If the quotation ends a sentence, put a full stop before the closing speech marks.
- ★ Start a new line for each new speaker.

RUBY'S RULES:

1. The words a person says always **begin** with a **capital letter**.

For example:

"**G**et up," the wolf said. (The wolf said, "**G**et up.")

2. The **question mark** or **exclamation mark** goes **inside the speech marks**.

For example:

"Oh help**!"** I squealed. "What do you want**?"**

3. If the **speech ends a sentence**, a **full stop** goes **before the closing speech marks**.

For example:

The wolf said**, "I** had better get you back**."**

4. Start a **new line** every time there is a **change** in the **person speaking**.

WOLF'S WHINES:

In the first draft Ruby wrote:

"Oh help. What do you want," I asked nervously. "Get up." the wolf said.

PUNCTUA'S POINTS:

It can be very confusing for the reader if dialogue is not punctuated correctly.

Top tip:

Start the speech using a **capital letter inside the opening speech marks**.

End the speech with a **comma**, **full stop**, **question mark** or **exclamation mark inside the closing speech marks**.

Tricky bit:

When the quotation is **interrupted**, it can get a bit tricky. Look at the following examples:

"**D**on't nip my hand again**,**" I shrieked.

If we break this quotation up:

"**D**on't**,**" I shrieked**,** "**n**ip my hand again."

Note: break up the speech using: (i) a **comma after the first words spoken**, (ii) a **comma after the speaker** and (iii) **no capital letter when the speech is restarted**.

11

Apostrophes

Section 1: To show possession (discovering what belongs to whom)

Section 2: To show possession (discovering if it's one or more)

Section 3: To show when two words have been joined together and some letters are missing

Section 4: Editing checklist

DOI: 10.4324/9781003190479-11

SECTION 1: TO SHOW POSSESSION (DISCOVERING WHAT BELONGS TO WHOM)

Apostrophes ,

Apostrophes are used to:

- ★ show possession (that something belongs to someone).

RUBY'S RULES:

An apostrophe (') + s **shows possession**.

It shows that **something** is **owned** by **someone** or is **connected** to **something**.

For example:

The basket belonging to Granny.

Granny**'s** basket.

The coat belonging to Ruby.

Ruby**'s** coat.

WOLF'S WHINES:

In the first draft Ruby wrote:

The wolfs' teeth.

She knew an apostrophe had to go somewhere *but* she clearly didn't know *where*.

She also wrote:

"Do not talk to strangers'."

PUNCTUA'S POINTS:

1. Wolfs' teeth

   There is only a **single** wolf. The **teeth belong** to **one wolf**.

   Who **owns** the **teeth**? The **wolf**.

   Add **'s** to wolf = **wolf's,** *not* **wolfs'**.

2. "Do not talk to strangers'."

   Does anything **belong** to the strangers? **No**.
   No need for an apostrophe.
   "Do not talk to **strangers**." (strangers is plural)

SECTION 2: TO SHOW POSSESSION (DISCOVERING IF IT'S ONE OR MORE)

Apostrophes

- Apostrophes are used to show possession.
- For plural nouns ending in 's' just add an apostrophe after the 's.'

RUBY'S RULES:

If something is owned by more than one person and the plural noun ends in 's':

For example:

The dung belonging to the **dragons**. (more than one dragon)

dragon**s** ends in '**s**.'

Add an **apostrophe** after the 's.'

The **dragons'** dung.

WOLF'S WHINES:

In the first draft Ruby wrote:

The trees's branches were knotted together.

The berries's juice was bright pink.

PUNCTUA'S POINTS:

The trees's branches.

There is **more than one** tree.

The plural of tree is **trees**. It ends in '**s**.'

As it already ends in 's,' just **add an apostrophe after the 's**.'

★ **the trees' branches**

Berries's juice.
The juice belonged to more than one berry.
The plural of berry is **berries**.
It already ends in 's' – **add an apostrophe after the 's**.'

★ **berries' juice**

What if the **plural** noun **doesn't end in 's**'? For example, **children**.

You need to add an **apostrophe and 's**': **children's room**

RUBY'S RULES:

If the something is owned by a **singular noun**, for example, **James**, which ends in **'s'**:

For example:

A trainer belonging to James

James already ends in **'s**.'

Add an apostrophe after the 's.'

Example:

★ **James' trainer**

Apostrophes

★ Apostrophes are used to show possession.

★ For singular nouns ending in 's' just add an apostrophe after the 's.'

WOLF'S WHINES:

In the first draft Ruby wrote:

Charle's house.

Iri's garden.

PUNCTUA'S POINTS:

Example: Charles' house
The house belongs to **Charles**.
Charles is **singular** and **ends in 's**.'
Add an **apostrophe after 's**'.

★ **Charles' house**

Example: Iris' garden

The garden belongs to Iris.

Iris is **singular** and **ends in 's**.'

Add an **apostrophe after 's**'.

★ **Iris' garden**

SECTION 3: TO SHOW WHEN TWO WORDS HAVE BEEN JOINED TOGETHER AND SOME LETTERS ARE MISSING

Apostrophes: contractions

Apostrophes are used to show when two words have been joined together.

- ★ Some letters are missing.
- ★ Missing letters are replaced by an apostrophe.

MISSING!

RUBY'S RULES:

When **two words** have been **joined** and **shortened**, apostrophes are used to **replace the missing letters**.

For example:

I'm (I **a**m); you're (you **a**re); she's (she **i**s); it's (it **i**s);

they're (they **a**re); he'll (he **wi**ll); can't (can**no**t); don't (do n**o**t); there's (there **i**s)

WOLF'S WHINES:

Thank goodness Ruby edited her story carefully. She got **it's/its** and **they're/their** terribly mixed-up, so her writing didn't make any sense.

She wrote:

The trees were bare. **They're** leaves were lying in a heap on the ground – dead, brown, shrivelled.

The wolf **didnt** look scary**. It's** eyes were amber and kind.

Over to you, Punctua! You're better at explaining this than me.

PUNCTUA'S POINTS:

When young writers are completing their first draft, initially they forget the apostrophe for contractions. It is, therefore, important that they have a list of contractions to check when they are editing.

Using the list, read through the draft and underline any of these words so that they can be checked for correct punctuation.

Editing checklist – contractions:

I'm, you're, he's, she's, it's, we're, they're, there's

I'll, you'll, he'll, she'll, we'll, they'll

Can't, didn't, don't, won't, couldn't, wouldn't

SECTION 4: EDITING CHECKLIST

Apostrophes

- it's/its
- they're/their
- you're/your

PUNCTUA'S POINTS:

Many young writers make the same mistake as Ruby with **its**, **theirs** and **yours**.

Remember that words like *his, her,* ***its****, your* and ***theirs*** that show **possession do not** have **an apostrophe**. They are an exception.

★ its (belonging to **it**)
★ it's (it **is**)
★ their (belonging to **them**)
★ they're (they **are**)
★ your (belonging to **you**)
★ you're (you **are**)

Example 1:

It's cold. (**It is** cold) ✓

Its cold. (**The cold belonged to it**) ✗

It's eyes were amber and kind. (**It is** eyes) ✗

Its eyes. (The eyes belonging to it) ✓

Example 2:

Their juice was pink and sticky. (The juice belonging to **them**.) ✓

They're juice was pink and sticky. (**They are** juice …) ✗

Example 3:

Your breath stinks. (The breath belonging to you.) ✓

You're breath stinks. (**You are** breath stinks.) ✗

Ruby corrected her work and changed it to:

The trees were bare. **Their leaves** were lying in a heap on the ground – dead, brown, shrivelled.

Its eyes were amber and kind.

Editing checklist: apostrophes					
Contraction		Contraction		Contraction	
I'm	I am	There's	There is	Can't	Can not
You're	You are	I'll	I will	Won't	Will not
He's	He is	You'll	You will	Don't	Do not
She's	She is	He'll	He will	Didn't	Did not
It's	It is	She'll	She will	Couldn't	Could not
We're	We are	It'll	It will	Wouldn't	Would not
They're	They are	We'll	We will		

12

Commas

Section 1: In a list

Section 2: To avoid misunderstandings

Section 3: To separate parts of a sentence

DOI: 10.4324/9781003190479-12

SECTION 1: IN A LIST

Commas in a list

- ★ Commas separate items in a list.
- ★ Use **and** to separate the last two items on a list.

RUBY'S RULES:

Commas separate items in a list to make the meaning clear.

Instead of saying:

Coffee **and** milk **and** tea **and** rubbish bags **and** fish.

Replace **and** with a **comma** except for the last item in the list.

Coffee**,** milk**,** tea**,** rubbish bags **and** fish.

WOLF'S WHINES:

If you don't use **commas to separate items in a list**, it can be very confusing.

Coffee milk tea disinfectant rubbish bags bread fish

Ruby couldn't understand the list and got:

Coffee, milk, tea disinfectant, rubbish, bags of breaded fish

PUNCTUA'S POINTS:

Commas are needed to make the meaning of a **list** clear and avoid any misunderstandings.

A comma can be used instead of **and**. It signals a slight **pause** between the **words or phrases** and helps the sentence to flow and not sound too jerky.

Use **and** to separate the **last two items** on a list.

The list should have been written:

Coffee, milk, tea, disinfectant, rubbish bags, bread and fish.

SECTION 2: TO AVOID MISUNDERSTANDINGS

Commas

- identify the person/people being addressed.
- make the sentence clearer and easier to read.
- avoid any misunderstandings.

RUBY'S RULES:

Commas are used to **separate the person/people** being identified **from the rest of the sentence**.

For example:

Don't tell anyone about me**,** Ruby.
Don't tell anyone about me Ruby.

WOLF'S WHINES:

I laughed until my sides were sore when I read the first draft of this story. At the end, when Ruby produced the picnic basket, she wrote that she had said:

"Let's eat Granny."

I bet that sent Granny's heart racing. She probably worried that Ruby had been spending too much time with wolves.

PUNCTUA'S POINTS:

Commas are needed to make the meaning clear and avoid any terrible misunderstandings.

Ruby needs to think carefully whether she is talking **to someone** or talking **about someone**.

Example:

"Let's eat Granny." With **no comma to separate eat from Granny**, this means that Ruby is talking **about eating Granny**.

"Let's eat, Granny." The **comma separates eat from Granny**, so Ruby is **talking to Granny** and saying that they should eat.

Example:

"Shall we leave Mum?" With **no comma to separate leave from Mum**, Ruby is talking **about leaving Mum**.

"Shall we leave, Mum?" The **comma separates leave from Mum**, so Ruby is **asking Mum** if they should leave.

SECTION 3: TO SEPARATE PARTS OF A SENTENCE

Commas to separate parts of a sentence

Commas:

★ separate parts of a sentence to help make the meaning clear.

★ add extra information to the main part of a sentence.

RUBY'S RULES:

A comma is used to:

★ **separate parts of a sentence** to help make the meaning clear.

★ **add extra information** to the **main message** of a sentence.

1. When joining two complete sentences, commas go:

   Between the **first complete sentence** and the **conjunction** (and, but, so, or).

   Example:

   I shouted for help**, but** nobody heard me.

2. When adding extra information to a complete sentence, commas go:

   Between the extra information and the main sentence.

3. The extra information often starts with conjunctions like:

   when, before, after, if, until, while, although

   Example:

   When it got dark**,** I couldn't find the path.

WOLF'S WHINES:

Indeed!

Ruby made this mistake throughout her first draft and it made it difficult to understand her writing.

She wrote:

When it got dark I couldn't find the path.

I shouted for help but nobody heard me.

PUNCTUA'S POINTS:

- ★ Too many short sentences can make your writing sound a bit jerky. They also slow the pace of the story because you keep having to stop all the time.
- ★ You can link your sentences and make them longer by:
  - a. **joining two complete sentences** together. For example, using conjunctions like **and**.
  - b. **adding extra information** to the **main part** of the sentence using conjunctions like **when**.

a. joining two sentences:

It got dark. I couldn't find the path.

These two complete sentences can be joined using **and**.

It got dark**, and** I couldn't find the path.

Note: there is a **comma before and** to link the two sentences.

b. adding extra information:

The reason Ruby couldn't find the path was **because** it was dark, so she could link the sentences by writing:

When it got **dark, I** couldn't find the path.

This time, Ruby is **not joining two complete sentences**. She is **adding some extra information** to the main message to make it clear why she couldn't find the path.

Main message – I couldn't find the path.

Extra information explaining why – When it got dark.

When it got dark doesn't make sense on its own. To make sense, it needs to be linked to the main message by a comma.

Note:

i. the conjunction **when** at the beginning

ii. the **comma after** the extra information

Tip: look out for the following **conjunctions** that help add more detail to your writing.

When, before, after, if, until, although

Appendix

Ruby's editing checklist level 1: punctuation

Ruby's editing checklist level 2: punctuation

Lord Lupus' challenge

Certificate: editing level 1

Certificate: editing level 2

RUBY'S EDITING CHECKLIST LEVEL 1: PUNCTUATION

	I confirm when I am editing, I check that:	✓
A.	**Sentences**	
1.	My sentences make sense.	
2.	My sentences end with a full stop.	
B.	**Capital letters**	
3.	My sentences start with a capital letter.	
4.	'I' has a capital letter.	
5.	Names of people and places have a capital letter.	
6.	Names of days and months have a capital letter.	
C.	**Questions and exclamations**	
7.	I put a question mark at the end of a direct question.	
8.	I put an exclamation mark to signal a surprise or outburst.	
D.	**Speech**	
9.	I put speech marks around the words being spoken.	
10.	I started a new line when the person speaking changes.	
11.	I started the speech with a capital letter.	
	Signature: Date:	

RUBY'S EDITING CHECKLIST LEVEL 2: PUNCTUATION

	I confirm when I am editing, I check that:	✓
A.	**Sentences**	
1.	My sentences are clear and easy to read.	
2.	I used a full stop, question mark or exclamation mark at the end of my sentences.	
B.	**Capital letters**	
3.	I used capital letters for 'I,' names of people, places, days and months.	
C.	**Apostrophes**	
4.	I used an apostrophe where something belongs to someone.	
5.	I used an apostrophe where letters are missing.	
6.	I haven't mixed up it's/its or they're/their.	
D.	**Commas**	
7.	I have used a comma to identify the person/people being addressed.	
8.	I have used commas to separate items in a list.	
9.	I have used commas to separate extra information from the main part of a sentence.	
	Signature: Date:	

LORD LUPUS' CHALLENGE

Correct the errors:

Have you been paying attention? Do you remember the mistakes I picked out and had to correct in Ruby's first draft? Test your knowledge by completing my challenge. *(You can always look back to check if you are not sure.)*

1. **Correct the passage so that it makes sense**
   I drifted in and out of sleep i had a strange feeling, that something or someone kept trying to wake me up i thought Id felt a warm breath on my cheek but i couldn't open my eyes to look
2. **Spot the comma splicing**
   i. Read the passage aloud.
   ii. Make a mark for each unit of sense.
   iii. Insert a full stop.
      a. Misty light shone through gaps in the trees, I was sure I had seen shadowy figures, they were dancing on the path in front of me.
      b. My fingers and face were stained, with sticky red juice, I licked my sticky fingers.
3. **Capital letters**
   Look for 'I,' names of people, places, days and months and insert a capital letter.
   a. The bow forest was on the outskirts of the village of stettal, on the other side of the river rath.
   b. Ruby said, "i go to visit granny every friday."
   c. i keep looking for lord lupus, but i haven't seen him since june.
4. **Question marks – yes or no?**
   Insert either **a question mark** or **a full stop** at the end of these sentences:
   a. What has made you so sick
   b. The wolf asked if he could see what was in my picnic basket
   c. Why don't you ever listen to your mother
   d. The wolf asked me why I never listened to my mother
   e. Granny asked me what had made me so sick
   f. Can I see what is in your picnic basket

5. **Exclamation marks**

   When would you use an exclamation mark?

   a.

   b.

6. **Punctuate the speech**

   a. Dragon's dung I yelled.
   b. What do you want I asked.
   c. I don't understand I said puzzled. A wolf ate my Granny and tried to eat my cousin.
   d. I really should have listened to my mother I moaned. By now, I was resigned to my fate. I'm lost in the forest and I have no energy to run I sobbed. I closed my eyes and rolled over.

7. **Apostrophes**

   i. Insert the apostrophe in the correct place.
   ii. Check its/it's and their/they're.

      a. The cakes and bread from Grannys basket are scattered all over the floor. I cant give them to her now.
      b. I dont know how long Ive been lying on the floor, but its getting dark. I cant see the wolfs mouth, but I think its smiling. I can see that it's eyes are an amber colour.
      c. The berries juice has dribbled down my face. My coat has big purple stains on it. Their going to be so cross when I get home. I wonder if I should go to Charles house to wash. Maybe not, its getting very dark.

8. **Commas in a list**

   i. Insert commas to separate the items on the list.
   ii. Explore what would happen if you put the commas in the wrong place.

I looked around at Granny's shopping. It was everywhere. There was soap cakes deodorant biscuits chocolate tins jelly toothbrush and hand sanitiser.

9. **Identifying the people being addressed**

   Read sentences a, b and c, and discuss questions 1–3 with a partner.

   a. Get the ingredients and we can prepare Merlin.
   b. Are you ready? Let's execute Granny.
   c. We've run out of time. We need to finish Ruby.
   d. "It's your turn to hide children," the teacher shouted.

Questions:

1. What do these sentences mean?
2. Where should the comma go?
3. How does inserting a comma change the meaning?

Certificate

EDITING LEVEL 1

awarded to

Name: ______________________

In recognition of your hard work in editing your writing.

Ruby Red & Punctua ______________________

____
Date

Certificate

EDITING LEVEL 2

awarded to

Name: ______________________

In recognition of your hard work in editing your writing.

Ruby Red & Punctua ______________________

______________________ *Date*